Charlotte
impressions

photography and text by **Robb Helfrick**

FARCOUNTRY
PRESS

Dedication

In memory of George Pfeiffer

*Dedicated to Becky, Steve, and Hannah —
wishing you great success and happiness
with your new life in Charlotte*

Front cover: The Charlotte skyline basks in the warmth of the
late-afternoon sun.

Back cover: Translucent mist from a circular fountain drifts over
seasonal flowers at Daniel Stowe Botanical Garden.

Title page: Spring colors paint the square at the historic meeting
of Trade and Tryon streets in Uptown Charlotte.

Right: The grounds of the Daniel Stowe Botanical Garden boast
a lovely assortment of colorful flora and flowing fountains.

ISBN 1-56037-310-5
Photography © 2004 Robb Helfrick
© 2004 Farcountry Press
Text by Robb Helfrick

For more information about our books write Farcountry Press, P.O. Box 5630,
Helena, MT 59604; call (800) 821-3874; or visit www.farcountrypress.com.

Created, produced, and designed in the United States. Printed in China.
08 07 06 05 04   1 2 3 4 5

Left: On the square, *Il Grande Disco* is a flawlessly balanced copper sculpture that stands as a monument to industry.

Far left: Geometric shapes are highlighted by morning sunlight in an aerial view of center city.

Right: Marshall Park's fountain spray reaches heights that seem to rival the Charlotte skyline.

Facing page: This Douglas DC-3 makes its home at the Carolinas Aviation Museum. The museum, which is located at the Charlotte/Douglas International Airport, houses a variety of both military and civilian aircraft. This particular airplane was built in 1942, restored in 1987, and brought to the museum in 1996. It still flies today.

Above: Tucked away in a quiet neighborhood, Wing Haven Gardens is a sheltered retreat for nature lovers and seekers of solitude. The three-acre greenspace was established in 1927 and contains both formal gardens and managed wilderness.

Left: Two boys seem spellbound as they peer into the Knight Rain Forest at Discovery Place Museum. The museum is a magnet for children, with exhibits that include the world's largest eyeball, an aquarium, and the Science Circus.

Right: As daylight fades, Charlotte's dynamic cityscape furnishes its own illumination.

Below: The lovely First United Methodist Church glows in golden light on a crisp winter morning.

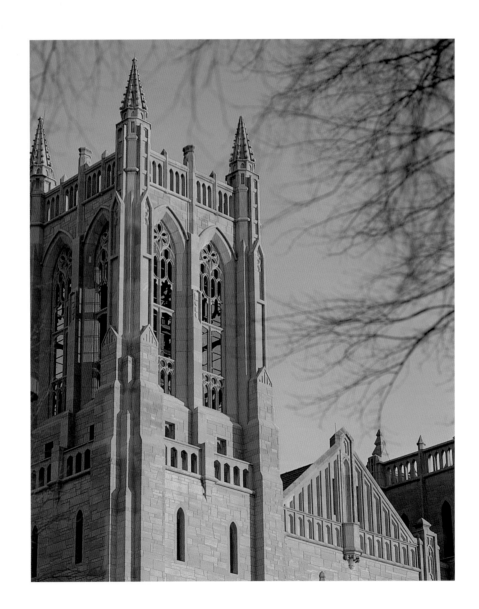

Above: Classic architecture enriches the campus of Davidson College, a liberal arts institution founded in 1837.

Left: Early light finds the Blumenthal Performing Arts Center in Uptown Charlotte. The center is a popular venue for contemporary music and the performing arts.

Right: The light-green hues of spring brighten a late afternoon at Freedom Park. The Park is a popular gathering place for those who enjoy the walking trail that circles the lake.

Below: A solitary horse grazes in a wildflower-filled meadow at Latta Plantation.

Left: Founders Hall is a sunlit shopping venue inside this vaulted-skylight atrium. The shops are connected to hotels and offices in center city through a system of walkways.

Below: The old Cabarrus County Courthouse is a signature landmark in Downtown Concord and is listed on the National Register of Historic Places.

Sailboats settle in for the evening at a marina on the shores of Lake Norman. With over 500 miles of shoreline, the lake has almost unlimited possibilities for scenic exploration.

Facing page: St. Peter's Episcopal Church is an elegant red-brick building nestled among trees on Tryon Street in Uptown.

Below: In the lobby of Bank of America Plaza, a fresco by artist Ben Long details the "making and building" of the structure, which was completed in 1992. This is Charlotte's tallest building and a symbolic center of the city's financial district.

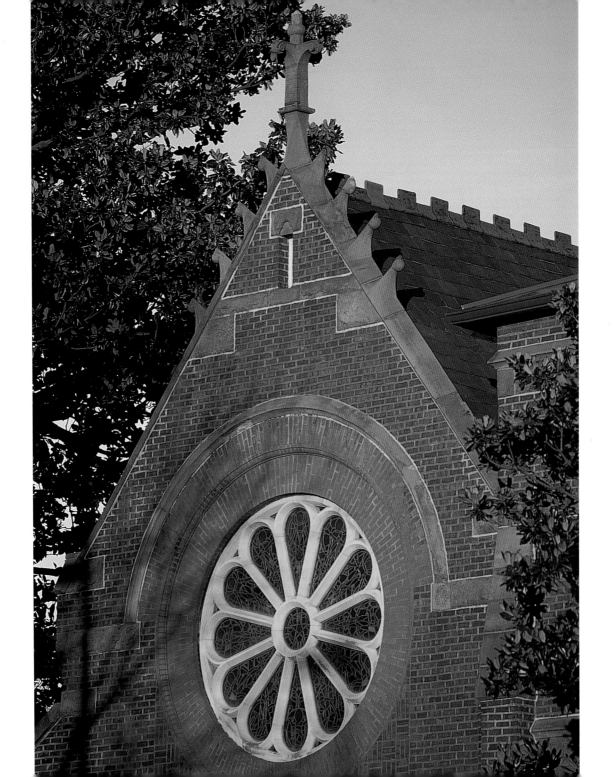

Left: Unique artwork and delicate dogwoods beautify the campus of the Metro School.

Far left: Charlotte's South End neighborhood is the place to find refurbished trolley cars that offer a nostalgic ride on the rails from Atherton Mills to Uptown.

Far right: Outside Spirit Square, colorful entrance signs give testament to the many forms of entertainment found inside. Two theaters and six art galleries offer venues for music, comedy, and dance events.

Right and below: Inside Belmont Abbey, a Benedictine monastery near Lake Norman, figures of devotion appear on backlit panes. Although they appear to be stained glass, these colorful windows were actually hand painted, then heat fused for even greater detail.

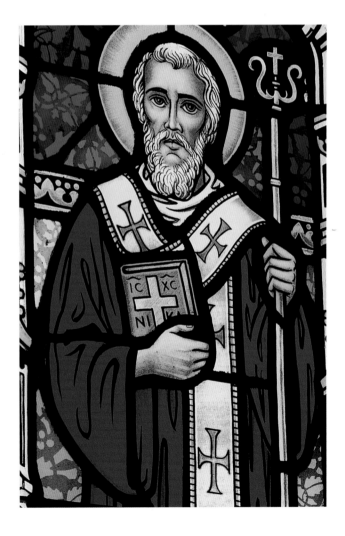

Right: The Hearst Tower is a recent addition to the Uptown skyline. This post-modern –style building stands 660 feet high and is Charlotte's second tallest building.

Far right: The reflective glass of a downtown office tower mirrors a multitude of hues from a blue Charlotte sky.

Left: A summer sunrise on the Catawba River promises pleasant weather for a day of leisure on the water.

Below: Tulips spring up in the Myers Park neighborhood, an elegant area of tree-lined streets and stately homes.

Right: This handsome rock house was once home to Hezekiah Alexander, one of Charlotte's early settlers. Alexander was a prominent Mecklenburg County citizen who arrived in the area circa 1767. His former home was restored in 1976 and stands on the grounds of the Charlotte Museum of History. It is the oldest surviving structure in Charlotte.

Below: A weathered wagon rests as shadows creep on a barn at Latta Plantation.

Left: The Charlotte Museum of History celebrates the area's past by utilizing artifacts and stories to create an understanding of the region's heritage and its impact on Charlotte's future.

Below: Spring comes into colorful bloom at the U.S. Courthouse on Trade Street.

Right: This stately clock tower is a recent addition to the beautiful campus of Queens University, a school originally founded as the Charlotte Female Institute in 1857.

Far right: Lake Norman is an upscale and picturesque setting for recreation and waterfront living.

Facing page: A panther guards the entrance to Ericsson Stadium, home of the NFL's Carolina Panthers.

Below: One of four monuments by artist Raymond Kaskey on the Charlotte square, *Commerce* commemorates the first documented gold discovery in America, which occurred in nearby Cabarrus County.

Above: On an opposite side of the square, *Future* is the second of four monuments that tell the story of Charlotte. It is symbolized by a mother holding her child.

Above: A backlit flower awakens with an early-morning stretch.

Left: Azaleas abound in Fourth Ward Park.

Right: A delicate detail found in Settlers' Cemetery is a modest measure of mortal recollection.

Far right: The handsome Charles Jonas Federal Building presents classical architecture on Trade Street.

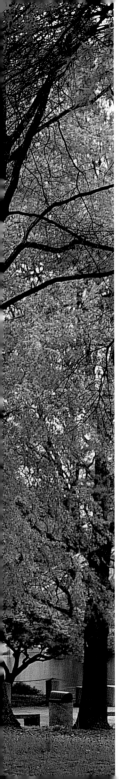

Left: On a gentle hill overlooking a pond, the legacy of Martin Luther King Jr. is remembered in Marshall Park.

Below: A sunlit pathway leads through a tapestry of tulips inside Concord's Memorial Garden.

Above: The spire of St. Peter's Catholic Church shares the Downtown skyline with The Ratcliffe, a contemporary residential complex that offers stunning views of the city.

Right: The inviting promenade of Hearst Plaza awakens at dawn.

Above: Panther colors fill the stands of Ericsson Stadium during an NFL contest.
On autumn afternoons, up to 73,000 fans cheer for their team.

Left: Ericsson Stadium is a state-of-the-art athletic facility that hosts the
Carolina Panthers, Charlotte's hometown football team.

Right: The grief felt from the loss of a loved one is frozen in time inside Elmwood Cemetery.

Facing page: A trio of architectural elements in Uptown Charlotte is centered on the Byzantine Dome of Spirit Square. The building, formerly the First Baptist Church, home to the McGlohon Theater, a signature performance space for the arts.

Above: All roads lead to Charlotte on a playful sign found on The Green, a new urban park in the heart of Uptown.

Left: The Hendrick Motorsports Museum is a NASCAR fan's dream. Inside this 15,000-square-foot facility the successful history of this prominent racing team is highlighted. Among the many former racecars found here is the one featured with Tom Cruise in the motion picture *Days of Thunder.*

Facing page: The sculpture *Helix/R* catches reflected light near the Charlotte square. The Uptown area is home to an impressive collection of expressive artwork that can be viewed on walking tours of the city.

Below: The early rays of the summer sun cast warm hues on Tryon Street buildings.

Right: Charlotte's gleaming skyscrapers stand tall in a view seen from the quiet surroundings of Fourth Ward Park.

Facing page: Outside Discovery Place, river birch trees are reborn in the springtime sun.

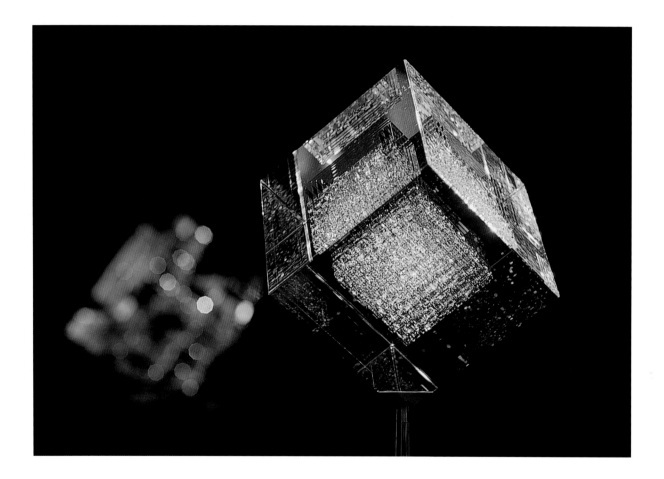

Above: The rich traditions of North Carolina crafts are showcased inside the Mint Museum of Craft + Design.

Facing page: The Afro-American Cultural Center has a lasting legacy of service as a nurturing and creative organization. The center celebrates and encourages the cultural, social, and artistic endeavors of Charlotte's African-American community.

Facing page: The historic Bost Grist Mill in Cabarrus County initially was powered by the waters of the Rocky River. After a severe storm a century ago, the structure was relocated a short distance away and now uses a pulley system for power generation. The mill still uses the original millstone to grind grain.

Below: A great horned owl keeps a vigilant eye on its surroundings at the Carolina Raptor Center. The center is dedicated to environmental education and the conservation of birds of prey.

Above: An American kestrel rests on the arm of its handler at the Carolina Raptor Center. Kestrels are the smallest falcons in North America and are also known as sparrow hawks.

Above: A multi-leveled fountain is shaded by the surrounding lofty buildings on the Charlotte square.

Left: The inviting arched entrance of the Charlotte Convention Center welcomes over half a million visitors a year.

Left: This yeoman's cabin at Latta Plantation recreates early nineteenth century backcountry life in North Carolina when cotton was the cultivated crop. Today, the property is a rustic and scenic Living History Farm.

Below: Golf is a popular outdoor pursuit around Charlotte.

Right: On the Charlotte square, the east-facing Kaskey sculpture represents *Industry.*

Far right: In a building conversion that has been successfully repeated at several creative venues in Charlotte, a former church has been transformed into the Tryon Center for the Arts.

Below: Playful figures are full of life in center city Charlotte.

Above: Dogwoods flower at Ribbon Walk Botanical Forest.

Left: Historic Rosedale Plantation, built in 1815, is one of the finest examples of Federal architecture in North Carolina.

Right: The last of four Kaskey sculptures on the Charlotte square, this figure represents *Transportation.*

Far right: President James K. Polk spent part of his childhood on his parents' 250-acre farm in present day Pineville, a suburb of Charlotte. Although the structures are not original to the Polk family farm, there are period buildings and furnishings here that give visitors a glimpse into the upbringing of America's eleventh commander in chief.

Left: The Charlotte area is the epicenter of NASCAR racing in the U.S. The Lowes Motor Speedway is a 1.5-mile superspeedway that hosts the Coca-Cola 600 and other major NASCAR race series events. Smith Tower is the portion of the speedway pictured here.

Below: A fusion of vintage and contemporary architecture coexists in Uptown Charlotte.

Left: Streetcar #1 is a restored trolley car displayed at the Charlotte Trolley Museum. It was retired and brought to Charlotte after faithfully serving on the streets of Piraeus, Greece.

Facing page: The South End area of Charlotte evolved as a textile-manufacturing hub along a busy rail line. The area was revived in the 1990s and the former mills and warehouses were transformed into colorful spaces for offices, shops, and restaurants.

Just a few steps from the bustling activity on Tryon Street, this courtyard in Transamerica Square is an oasis in the heart of Uptown Charlotte.

After a drive into the country past farms and open fields, visitors to the
Cowan's Ford Wildlife Refuge can enjoy quiet natural surroundings.

Left: Warm sunlight creates a sculptural silhouette at Trade and Tryon.

Below: In 1799 the discovery of a large gold nugget (reported to have weighed 17 pounds) was found on Little Meadow Creek by young Conrad Reed. Conrad's father John, unaware of the true nature of this discovery, used the yellow rock as a doorstop for three years. After realizing the rock was a prized commodity, John Reed sold it and started his own mining business. A gold rush soon followed, and as a result North Carolina would lead the nation in gold production until California's more famous gold rush surpassed it in 1849.

Right: A Canada goose pauses for a reflective rest in Marshall Park.

Far right: Myers Park is a lovely neighborhood that was once home to the banking and textile leaders of the early 1900s. It remains a prestigious Charlotte address today.

Below: The American Freedom Bell is a seven-ton symbol that was presented to the city by the Belk Foundation. It rests on the grounds of the Charlotte Museum of History.